The Day Is Quieter Than Night

Also by Karen Hubbard

Rain (2006)

The Day
Is Quieter Than
Night

Poems by **Karen Hubbard**

L'Orange Press
West Orange, New Jersey

Copyright ©2012 by Karen Hubbard
Printed and bound in the United States of America

All rights reserved. No part of this publication maybe reproduced or stored in a retrieval system or transmitted in any form or by any means, including electronic, mechanical, photocopying, recording, without the prior permission of the author. Any inquiries are to be made to the publisher.

First Edition
ISBN
978-0-578-09957-6

L'Orange Press
West Orange, New Jersey
lorangepress@yahoo.com

Photography and Book Design by Karen Hubbard

Acknowledgements

I am thankful to those whose support and guidance made this book possible. Firstly to my writer friends Pina Pipino, Maryann Seibert, Marilyn Mohr, Norma Miller, Nina Ziv, Georgianna Hart, and others. I am grateful to Michael Lally and his workshops, which helped to hone my "voice". And most especially to my daughter whose love has helped to sustain me.

Appreciative acknowledgement is made to the following publications in which several of these poems first appeared: *Amelia, A Stone Unturned (Anthology), Austin Downtown Arts Magazine, Maultrommel, Open Doors (Anthology), Promethean, Rain, and Shot Glass Journal.*

For Kelly and Allison

Contents

Chicago

History / 15
The Erector Set / 17
1970 / 19
The Bus Ride / 21
Oasis / 23
Clean / 24
Colors / 25
Naming / 26
Scene From Voyages On Chicago
      Elevator Trains / 27
The Benton Women / 28
These Women / 29
Hurricanes / 30
The Kiss / 32
To The Poet Who Introduced Me To Robert Bly / 33
Winter Poems / 35
Chicago Chronicles / 36
Sketches From A Notebook / 39
The Borders Of Love / 40

Cities Afar

Mexican Coffee / 45
Puerto Plata / 46
Barcelona / 47
In Madrid / 48

Berlin / 50
Dublin / 53
Edinburgh / 55
Geneva / 56
Italian Impressions / 57
Le Hameau Du Passy / 59
A Day With Debussy / 61
Daydreaming / 62
Discovery Is Fragile / 63
The Tango / 64
The Plains / 65
Odysseus / 67
Home Again / 69

New York

Moonlight Drive / 73
Sunrise / 74
At The MET / 76
The Dancer / 77
Tenugui / 78
On Viewing Alfred Stevens' The Bath / 79
Metamorphosis / 80
Kites / 82
Nameless / 83
Every Poet Has A Poem Like This / 84
Portrait / 85
Wandering Amidst Her Garden Of Wild Flowers / 86

Poets In The Burrito Bar / 87

On Reading Frank O'Hara –Lunch Poems / 89

String Theory / 90

Sublime And Beautiful (On Reading Kant) / 91

Cento – Autumn / 93

From Where Does It Come? / 94

In My Garden / 95

Narrowing / 96

Órga Leannán (Golden Lover) / 97

Porcelain / 98

Snow Angels / 99

Sought Music *Ex Nihilo* / 100

Spirit Line / 101

Wandering Men / 102

Winter Is The Reason/ 103

New York Postcards / 105

Holding A Pear / 107

Parties / 109

History

older women travel, sometimes
in the morning
taking their time
climbing onto each step
one shoe first, then another
while the bus driver yells
"Come on lady, hurry up"

grandmamma never let speed
stand in her way
her agile movements from kitchen
to day time soap operas
defied time

my history lies buried in her
curled together, she would talk
about anything, comb her long hair
reminding me of an old native Indian princess
except her grandmother was an African slave

she would talk of Papa
and his flight from the law
and her love
and how the rain poured down her back
waiting in the mud

but there she stood
holding all reason in one brief touch

(a white man had threatened her chastity)
Papa had a gun
they said Papa had murdered

later, he gave in
was paroled and died
accidentally
against a Chicago basement wall

"life was hard sometimes"
she said, "on a Mississippi farm"

The Erector Set

at ten, i wanted
an erector set for Christmas
but
received a doll instead.

my mother, a tomboy from Jackson, Mississippi
wanted her daughter to be a real "girl".

the doll was blond, blued-eyed
equipped with pink hair rollers and
portable bouffant dryer – the kind
that came with a chair.

i simply wanted an erector set.
my hands feel useful
when things connect.

my brothers, knew i hated dolls
would light their blond tresses,
smells of burning plastic
would permeate the house
from time to time.

for some reason the following year,
she gave me a chemistry set
with test tube holders, chemicals, Bunsen burners,
chemical methods.
until an experiment flew out of its glass container
and landed on my little sister's forehead.

"see" she said. "see what you've done,
i told you"
and then closeted a career in chemistry.

it was only water and salt
but my sister still shows a slight
discernible scar.

1970

downtown Lake Forest, Illinois
a college town
was culture shock for me
an inner city Chicago kid

head shops
lined the street across from the train station
but it was 1970 and music was hip
like joni
smoky cannabis
filled rooms of coffee houses

upscale Marshall Fields department store
loomed nearby with five stretch limousines
parked outside

in downtown Chicago, i had always roamed
Marshal Fields at Christmas
animated scenes in the outside
picture windows
watching the Lionel train tracks and trains
whistle by, while eating Frango mints

it's not easy to walk
the streets at night, in a town frozen by the lake
and one day to be filmed for "Ordinary People"

i could not bring myself
into its grand stores

somehow, it was inconsistent with
my large afro and Angela Davis glasses
turban and African robe
while standing real close listening to Alice Coltrane
on our college stage
when she played, wistfully smiling
  "my favorite things"
remembering John

The Bus Ride

somewhere
between Cheyenne and North Platte
he sits
next to me
and turns on his light.

minute cities
flicker in
the premature night
as we ride the Chicago-bound
Greyhound bus.

he's headed for Des Moines
and laughs with burly
mid-western resonance
as he talks of monthly
bus passes and nickel
trolley rides
in San Francisco.
i learn of family
and hard times
and how a man would
cut
the spoiled parts
from pickings in back of
Henry's grocery store.

he's retired
and says, "i don't sleep much these days.
can't live if you're asleep."

later, in the bus depot
goodbyes are made
and i return to my seat
turn my head
fall to sleep
once more
as the bus moves on.

Oasis

we sit before these words
in a little brown church
"blessed are the peacemakers"
inscribed on the stained glass window
while eating poetry and pasta

i had thought
a new century would bring promise
but in these past years
it takes more than strength
to remember all the death dates
mother
father
aunt and uncle
friends with breast cancer
HIV and first cousins

i live my seconds
hoping that somewhere near
when the edge
of the desert meets
the edge of a sea
an oasis
will be found

but i find
sulfured-smoke
ashes
wailing on the wall
for all those remembered
in
another
death date

Clean

i look around me
it is clean, like my mother's

she, the poorer relation
could never get it quite right
but her house was spic and span
she would polish
the soles of baby shoes until frigid white.

i learned early to shine our floors
and sit quietly on the bathroom floor
to lock out intruders
fantasies soared, some not so pretty

and throughout the house the wind
would whistle.

Colors

colors have always mattered
like   brown   deep amber
white ropes hanging   stained red

these days conjure a multitude of hues
the kind tied with fear
difference

Naming

my mother's name was Miriam
she was always lost in the adjectives of her life
never knowing
that it had become a poem

did your mother know that you were a prophet
did she know of your visions in her womb
did she unconsciously perceive
an older biblical sister of yours,   Maryam

Maryam, who foretold the wonders of Moses
who foretold the splendor of the Promised Land
and like her brothers, never stood on its earth

my mother saw heavenly visions, long pilgrimages
during her many weekends of liquor and cigarettes

she knew she had come to that point
where the waters open
red and angry

i knew she would walk surely across them

Scene From Voyages On Chicago Elevator Trains

this pharaoh

exiled from the Nile's flood

slept

while grave robbers

pilfered pockets

hunting

the meager treasures

that were to set sail

in eternal voyage

with an old drunk

The Benton Women

hand held memory
this photograph
five young women
lean close to one another
café au lait   like me
i am in the tiny creases of their faces   strong like them
one vibrantly laughs
hunches her back   stretches out her arms
stands in dance mode
the fairies must have painted
those freckles   on her nose

These Women

we women
sit around a worn oak table   coming and going
each one   one at a time

we collect together   little things
tears from failed relationships
newborn baby's breath

when anguish
reaches with outstretched arms
we are
for one another
umbrellas in the snow

Hurricanes

> *When the hurricane gets inside*
> *Nobody knows what color light is going to take to illuminate*
> *The prodigious appearance of the lovely monsters it creates*
>   -Roger Gilbert-Lecomte (1938), *Come the Hurricane*

i
learned too young
not to ever look
for hurricanes

displacement of happiness
came more than often

tempests hurled my mother
no chance for rescue

so
when does a hurricane get inside?
i try not to remember

my arms
wrapped tightly about my chest
will not allow hurricanes
to enter

i try
to fall into the exuberance of passion
hold back any lovely monsters

but the color of your voice
lights
this inescapability of darkness

The Kiss

you light tea candles
carry them to me
dimming iridescent lights and explore each
kiss

and said "don't like me too much"

i wanted to encircle the long strands of your dark hair
into my consciousness
a madwoman from Chicago water

words can be simple
love in these moments
complex as
my father's
or my brother's
who spends endless nights
denying the streets, the needle, the kiss
the warmth of abandoned cars
another day

To the Poet Who Introduced Me to Robert Bly

you found me sitting in the back, of a
wood paneled room,
lit by snow falling outside
the stained glass windows
– a poetry reading in Hyde Park

remembering now, while
i drink warm green tea
as the rain falls
in this premature spring

you were tall,
with a long grey ponytail
we talked all night, you had left
wife, children, job
to live among piles of books and poems
one room

you ached to be free

and would give your poems
on Chicago street corners,
to anyone

take me to ethnic dives
and downtown readings

– mesmerized,   i listened to Bly's fingering
of strings, quiet poems
images of snow birds and forests

you had wanted me to,
love you

but now, i can't remember
your   name

Winter Poems

1

we are riding
to downtown Chicago
(unless the bus gets turned around)
packed together, rigid bodies
touching in mass transit
the city has painted its eyelids
with arctic white
and all the women
hide their beauty behind
woolen veils

2

it hasn't snowed for days
but the reflection from raindrops
on glass windows
wakes you to death flirting
with the darkness
which hangs as a backdrop for the rain,
rain drops that cascade the transition
from flurried snowflakes to old age

Chicago Chronicles

1
The Loop

in the crook of my neck
strands of your dark hair
nestle
while your brow whispers across my lips

night hawks glide above
i am home again

2
Hyde Park

from the window tops of her T-bird
Dire Straits cruised at 50mph
along South Lake Shore Drive
winding our way down to Jimmy's neighborhood bar
home of poets   philosophers
drunks and Wild Turkey whiskey

3
Lake Forest

over looking
the iced stairs
at the edge of the snow crusted lake
the Spanish Castle weeps

4
Lake Michigan

the day is coldly bleak   wet
as i drive to downtown Chicago
homecoming
walking though the Aqua Lakeshore Apartment
as if in Gaudi waves

then i sit   listen to your Franck strings
sonatas   snowflakes that melt on my tongue
while thunder outside shudders

5
Old Town

on Sundays my father would take me to crowded
jazz bars
while i licked my fingers   red from
the spiced shrimp of Navy Pier
beats filled our bodies
he'd ask "girl, do you know?"

but how could i
at sixteen know
the many paternal half-brothers and sisters
the death of my mother's alcohol abused heart
the lingering sweetness of my newborn child

Sketches from a Notebook

1
he sat on the floor of the bookstore,
quietly between Classics and Biology
he was deliciously young
long black hair tied Japanese style

2
on the burgundy wall
of the Sultry Scissors hair salon
white candles dripped

the salon was part of an ancient history   of
black beauty salons
and barbershops
for gatherings,   gossip
the latest sweeping and impossible looking hair dos

the Isley Brothers crooned above from the speakers
while a line of soon to be styled women   (and lately men)
were strategically placed to gaze
on the red, white and blue poster

"Obama 08"

The Borders of Love

Between two mouths in a kiss
Windowglass.
               -Roger Gilbert-Lecomte (1938)

Dear A.:

This is the first letter i have written to you in more than 10 years. It seems that i've taken to reducing our closeness into memories as if definitions of familial applied only to the mind. But of course, you know this, we are sisters. i would have sent a poem instead. These days - the rigidity of lines/words are a struggle and are beyond capture.

My friend D. had a birthday recently and i took her to the Village. This winter is far fiercer than i remember for new york. i've always laughed at the vulnerability of new yorkers. You and i were molded from chicago ice panes and wind. Anyway, we walked for hours before the movie. In and out of dark graffiti, streets housing Soho galleries. Men dressed in village black and women hiding their beauty behind smudged eye liner marks and red red lipstick. We wandered into a used bookstore and while i scanned the poetry section, i heard conversations reminiscent of ones i avoided long ago when i studied literature. Like Artaud, i have at times found words meaningless, painful. i prefer the simplicity of syllables as in a child's picture book. Each phrase exact, lucid.

And then, i saw him. His eyes were dark and peered out from the page - sinister and he knew me. i stood there holding his book in my hands, reading as if each word was written to me, through me, in me. Obscurity of a young drugged-out french poet, dead at 36, long before i was born. But i knew his eyes, he would have known me. The chatter down the aisle served as a backdrop, as all life suddenly a mute panorama. if love could be served as such, then, i would have fallen. Okay, you probably would tell me, i understand it's only fantasy. But to be haunted by mirrors.......

i know that i have fallen into the black mirror. Last summer i fell and now only in this coldness, have i made my ascent. Examining a love whose borders brought the spiritual to ignite my eyes. Finding myself, loathing myself, loving again - and all these things could be dismissed so easily. love him, not in love, and love as carefully as i love my own child. Being out of the mirror, i see him, clearly in myself. The reality of the windowglass.

Threads, spun glass, reaching from me and as fragile as the quiet reading of a young man alone in the Angelica cafe. i watch him turn pages from the corners of my eyes. My red lips burning and my friend noticing that everyone except her is wearing black. His dark hair brushing against the pages - i turn to look at him but he has gathered his purchases and left the room. i return to my poet - in my hands his eyes burn red.

i dream from the mirror. The browness of my body wraps and absorbs the reflected color of snow. ice melts on my fingertips as i lick each one - transmuting winter. Remembering our mother's journey into the snow and the distillations and the visions. She protects me now, pulling my arms, no salvation when there is no fall. And my knowledge comes in double. you and i are sisters, but he and i were born together, seconds apart. Glass threads separating us but apparent always. And our thoughts as lyrical as the boundaries which keep us.

i enjoyed the movie. i am well.

    yours,
    K.

Mexican Coffee

grey plumes of sky loomed ahead
BOMBEROS was painted bold on the angry truck before us
"a word that sits thick on the tongue," my friend says
as our taxi passes the border   Jalisco to Nayarit

invisible iguanas rustle their presence
in this too familiar foreign jungle foliage

the evening is lit by coffee flambé
which the waiter pours from one silver dish to another
and then back again
the taste so warm   but far too sweet

Puerto Plata

the slightly sweet milk
from green coconuts by the sea
cool

i look through
your dark long lashes
and grey eyes
– you whisper
"let's go to Santiago"
i hesitate

we dance the merengue
our brown bodies
close and slow

your first kiss
passionate
under the whirling colors
while fans try
to cool

but the dance
and the music
keep us warm

Barcelona

i walk to sacred spires
that reach for   a spoken metaphor
like expectations   happiness

underfoot,   the geometric waves   tiles of life
pave this road

passion cascades into flamenco

In Madrid

the fortune teller said, "i'll light two candles"
(while colorful saints and virgin statues trembled)
"one white, one black. there is troubled rain ahead,
his path once parallel crosses yours".

the monastery on top of the ancient hillside
drinks in the rain but offers no sanctuary.
i light a white candle for you
as have many laced women for love,
to glow within the crimson holder-
only 25 pesetas for the box.

rain,
my talisman follows us into the city.
only to release a piercing sun
through our umbrella in the Plaza Mayor.
we cry, "la cuenta, por favor".
languishing in the heat,
we drink sangria
and eat tapas under Hemingway's sky.

the pebbled rectangular courtyard,
strolling minstrels with mandolins
unchanged in tenor since before the wars.
but the pigeons sense the dangers of ghosts
at the end of siesta,

fly head on towards the large clock at the top of the Plaza –
maybe it was the wails of human heretics

or the screams of ole!
while men senselessly stare down the beast.

it does not change,
beautiful woman still laced and alluring –
"come, do you like what you see señor?
you need only to lift my skirt to dance with me".
hand painted fans, are their dark eyes.
he clicks his heels, arches his back
and tosses his long red cape
around her shoulders.

Berlin

1
nearly raining
sitting here near
a bright neon kneipe
a half-hour from
desolation and the wall –
torn down now
the dark skies
pleading
nichts zu lieben dich
and beneath the quiet politeness
disturbing all sensibility
is the rage

it is nearly
raining, and cars speed by –
some American melodies
down the Mommsen Strasse
luxurious –
young Berliners and cigarettes
and bier drunken heads
upon bar counters
insensible to movement

the meaning of this,
i see in the clearness

of your dark hair –
though different continents,

makes possibilities
of all of my
sentiments
and softens the contrasts
in a far city

2
in love with the city's
Strasse
talking
sitting beneath the large schutz
rain falls

the garden lit
with small iridescent
light bulbs
the kind we use
at Christmas or holiday parties
your ghost
i see, walking underneath
the veranda
feel you next to me
though distances

argue
how can she love
this man, this city
the wall has been
torn down
a memory of broken
unkindness
when love should reach
not
across continents
but inches

Dublin

1
it is raining in this
windy medieval
harbor town
i search for a poem
in the center
of this city

downstairs at Brogan's pub
where walls littered with faded half-colored posters
rain seeps
into the beer stained wood
and onto the floor

we huddle closer

it is familiar here
home among poets
from different lands
we sing poems
in hip-hop slam and traditional

i hear the lyrics of a one man Kavanagh
tattered and tall
" write from your dreams
we are both art and aesthetics

our words reflect the poetry
in living"

the old Dublin Joyce knew
felt in full

2
no mind is safe to walk the red
cobbled-stone streets of Grafton to
the Book of Kells

a journey from darkness
into light

half-pissed last night
my head is full
the seagulls cry to stop
but the call of this book
is as wanton
as a black-haired Irish beauty

3
it is still raining
we envision ourselves
as prisoners, like Wilde
we invent our tents of life
our blue skies

Edinburgh

from the sidewalk
i hear these words, he is simply singing
"love is larger than life"

drenched,
the rain drops on my lips
bead
like quivering moths
searching for daylight

my steps are lost, here in these narrow
streets, this city is old
older than my hunger
older than my sighs

Geneva

i am broken
& my edges are uneven
but form a circle

i search in the old town
for passion is vision
i sit in the Café La Clemence
as the dimming sunlight filters
espresso and captures a moment

i lose myself in this crowd,
just another anonymous woman
as the waiter asks "what is your pleasure, madam?"

i am intrigued by intensities
i am dizzy from the cognac as it slips
past my lips into my mouth
vertigo

Italian Impressions

suddenly lost
hunting an entrance along the stone walls
of Lucca
dreams are only images
we are afraid of
my daughter says
or was it my niece?
as they lay together
for the night
while the fan hums across the room
to keep cool dreams

i retrace
my steps in droplets,
collecting
mountain water flowing
into aqueducts to Pisa
and the moon-littered Arno

brilliant red poppies bursting
along the rails to Florence
suddenly stepping into sculpture
lucious hillsides,
cypress and olive trees

dream dancing
in these mists
i become
so
easily
stilled

Le Hameau du Passy

bonsoir,
the pigeons coo
in the stillness
of this early evening
which is like a soft
and slightly sweet port.

the vines of ivy
not as old as this city
crawl the cracks
of the plastered courtyard walls,
aching to kiss the red flowers
in the box outside my window.

the Eiffel Tower glows,
a few steps beyond
in the sky and from the Seine.

a Benedictine monk, a refugee from California –
as he gazed into his dark Irish beer said,
"the plans of God are beyond our grasp".
he sighed, smiled
as he stroked the earring in his right ear.
"grace", i said,
"is only second place to faith
which can be

as elusive
as a first kiss".

yet, sitting here,
writing from my window,
knowing in other times
and other streets, poets
or otherwise
have come to a glass of portwine
in one hand and a pen in the other.

the tears of life
pour
like the river Seine
or ink across the page.

A Day with Debussy

in autumn, the silvered sunlight
questions
her grey clouds
but smiles to turn
to listen
to the music
as it sweeps through the
nearly bare
trees

Daydreaming

flying to california
i dream
there is something about your smile
that engulfs the room
and everyone   watching lazily in
afternoon rain, as it torments the sidewalk
(i don't know what there is about
       dreaming in the day – maybe
       your eyes or a thought of a kiss
which impels me so – i only know
that the day is quieter than
       night)

moonlight claws my mind and heart,
and like ancient japanese women
waiting behind bamboo silken screens
my heart blazes, and cannot be
calmed by the night
(why is there so much mystery
       some know the meaning of dreams,
       as each curl of your hair
tumbles into memory and
explodes into my
       day –)

Discovery is Fragile

the week before my surgery
they read the names of the dead
on a grey   bitterly   cold   day

next day i sat under a silver strobe
surrounded by warm red brick walls
in a café
and tried not to look into his eyes
as he said "my life is too complicated"

Molière once wrote, "the great ambition of women
                    is to inspire love"

somehow all these things passed through
as they wheeled me into the operating room

now i'm in recovery

The Tango

intricate steps
crisscross turns, in this
dance, your arms
our eyes locked tight open
in tango
suddenly remembering
my eyes in shutters
(the taste of
           your lips)
sensuous and slow, each turn
thighs brush so
fleetingly light
prelude and fiery
passion

The Plains

winds
rip through

ghost-like echoes
shake roof tops

so many new voices now
hungry moans chase us

no longer   the ancient rattles   ancient chants

children
eyes sunken
deadly threats in the night
lull them to sleep

they sometimes try to push aside old carrions
who look with recognition
in their eyes

as we walk among the homeless
the hungry moans chase us
ancient rattles, ancient chants
elude us

if only we could restore the plains
if only we could shake the rattle
would there be
fewer voices?

Odysseus

my cane transforms the reality
of a full moon
into long walks of webbed caverns
waiting monk-like
to taste exuberance
i see her fingers unwind the colored threads

Penelope sits
as she unwinds each layer
my body drags across the floor
among the sweat drenched dance shoes

i throw back my hood
consume
arias of thoughts   recalling
brief shuttered mornings
wind inhaling
leaves of trees

i see a dreaming Penelope
her thoughts
undone upon the loom

she finds my love
as slender
indiscernible fibers
which wrap slowly   slowly
within all of my inconsistencies
and so   i wait

for   her

Home Again

i feel
like the time i stood before
the wall
after it came down,
standing before the wide desolate streets of East Berlin

now driving down the
garden state, the radio sings
"we've all come to look for America"

suffering is offered as a kiss

underground, our emotions never surface
to face the dead, lying on street corners
waiting to live each second from the cracks
of the sidewalk

road kill
but of a different kind

Moonlight Drive

air warmed by March
blew past windows of her car

here, there is less than a quartered moon
near the Hudson river
as the woman checks the nervous
dark brown strands of hair
through squinted eyes
in the light of that moon,
she smoothes the kinky waves
and thinks:
driving in Chicago
speeding past the near lifeless lake
is much more than this

philosophies in life
viewed at night
as the drive comes closer to a
moon
voluptuous in ruby lips
pale
as she drives closer, and then
even closer
eclipsed into sadness

Sunrise

somewhere
an old man sits
watching
a river

but i sit watching
the night

iridescent candles
pierce

humanity
flickers madly
against the evening

every night
this neon life
sends me secretly
off to sea
there is no reason
for resonance to linger
city nights
exist for themselves

at sunrise, each light fades

it is enough to sit

and watch

as the pattern

in last night

changes with the day

At The MET

he leaned, his tan leathered fingers
gripped the cane as he
bent over but dared not touch
the black lacquered   jeweled chest
and tilted his beige fedora sideways
in an old world gesture

sometimes
we are told to eat
but there is a thin veil
between heaven and earth

sometimes
i wish i could see the nothing
in nothingness
the more
in timelessness

The Dancer

she stands behind
gated plum blossoms
illuminated rice paper

she grasps tight
the folded partition
to move it slightly
then in wanton beckoning
the other hand
touches slightly above
her breast

stillness wrapped the cherry blossoms
inside her kimono

her red,
lips parted

her hand suddenly fluttered
a fan

– a butterfly
the half-opened fan
falls

hard

Tenugui

wisteria and
the pine tree enveloped in a kiss
i wrap your scarf
around me,
a lavender tenugui
longing like the vine for the tree
patient and ardent
waiting for the next touch
of your lips

On Viewing Alfred Stevens' The Bath

soft peach roses precariously hang
from her fingertips
on the side of the enameled bath tub

the black pocket watch
lying in the white soap dish on the wall
had stopped

her arm tilts behind her head
eyes lost
in the measure of time

Metamorphosis

1

emerging slowly, crawling into the world
part of name changing
husband or lover, encasements
crawling out of the molt
struggling to breathe in a newness
loving a man so completely
to be twins or lovers
never really mattered
i've made such proclamations, reformations
breathing in his warmth
i've painfully moved, snake dancing
inching
holding my arms about me
part of name changing
eyeing snake charmers
holding my breath to steady his
and the dark, dark truth
yet still lies between
identical shedding of skins

2

time tonight, walking, wandering
manhattan air blasting against
my cheeks
young men pushing shopping carts

the sidewalks have become
grocery stores, and trash cans

house their wares
and me, holding my heart warm
i've just emerged
newborn smell, silky softness
jazz beats, bursting out
of the nearby cafe, as i walk
holding my heart warm
my hands have mittens

i have changed my name, lost my twin
the music in the shopping carts
in the cafe, in our newly formed souls
have found him again
and all the proclamations
and all the shedding
and all the dark truths
fraternal in keeping, to be twins or lovers
does not really matter

my breath is now mine alone

Kites

a long thin line on my brown skin
almost gone now, but
i remember at
thirteen
sliding across the razor sharp snow
losing my mother's hands
as she lifted   waved them
kites
in the sky

no soothing touch
just words

but words are like kites
they can be waved away
palms upward

Nameless

after glasses of red Zinfandel
my head clears as i sip
orange dulce tea
in Sweet Basil Café

The People say "do not whisper the names
of our dead"
leave their treasures in dusty pawnshops

nameless,   but not forgotten spirits
roam mesas   aspen   deserts

they follow me
linger here in my head
as i try
but cannot say your name

Every Poet Has a Poem Like This

your body moves towards me
arms warmly slightly touching
then suddenly retracting
like brilliant phrases
evaporating
irretraceable

my brain delves deep
through its layers to bring you into
this wonderful spring air

my fingers touch the tips
of yours
which instinctively   pull back

Portrait

i said to her
"once written
a poem belongs to no one"
she is shrewd
invents
her life as it folds
she writes poems
of social injustices
she is of that age
of sultry jazz
later, bra burning
but is tied
lovingly
to upcoming marriage vows
homemade pastries
she
is the paradox
i think

Wandering Amidst Her Garden Of Wild Flowers

– for Patricia Fillingham

she once told me,
"I started writing poetry
when I felt something
that needed to be said"
as she made tea
in the well worn kitchen
a place for soirées   and
collections of poets and engineers
expanding into the outer rooms
like the big bang
amid the wall to wall lining of books

always intrigued,
she would listen to the voices
of things
like wild flowers
and   found smooth stones,
thrown carelessly by the wind

she embraced the growing wildness of her body
not surrendering
but uncovering new discoveries
as she walked around her garden
as words fierce
sometimes softly humorous
tumbled from her

Poets in the Burrito Bar

we sat in the bar,
deep back
in a smoky dim lit room
on a corner
of the city on Church street.
the street was dark
but could not hide the funky sixties décor
or the ravished face of the city outside.

we sat drinking margaritas,
i drank warm lime-laced Coronas
while smoky colored plastic beads
hanging in the doorway
sensuously danced
with each passerby.

slowly i watch in freeze frame
    (my body lying on your bed.
    your fingers encircling each breast,
    while the smoky crystal beads
    that dangle from my neck
    watch)

each poet

had some secret to divulge.

notes of memories,

words

are eaten in full

like spicy black beans.

On Reading Frank O'Hara –Lunch Poems

this is not lunchtime
amazing whiffs of coffee - espresso
my addiction
since cool early summer evenings in Italy,
strolling by the Arno and lover's clasping arms
in the filtered music of the club by the river.
i found coffee at twenty-seven
during the long hours of chemical formulas and ee cummings.
who ever said poets are never scientists
have never tasted you or a sprinkle of cinnamon in the morning,
pure philosophy.
even now in coffee bookstore bars,
anonymous men meet anonymous women
to sip
first love.

String Theory

grown weary of resistance
i move towards him   in syllables
each one a separate string

the space between them vast
and yet in secret places   they collide
explode into galaxies

when i think of his lips
i try to seduce him with cummings   William Carlos Williams

but he is   too young   sharp   hard sculpted
and wants to love like   Bukowski

Sublime and Beautiful (On Reading Kant)

i
search the eyes
of a thousand faces
pushing time
waiting
in its terror

i fall
into the deep pools
your brooding eyes

nothing is ever certain
and the truth
like time and space
shifts

love
once beautiful
now sublime

morning air
has fantasies of you
and intoxicates

i drink the
lusciousness of your lips
i drown in your mouth

i look
through the night
for a sign of you

for the night sky is a landmine, here
for only
this moment

Cento – Autumn

Whether or not we can read you,
We can feel
A sense of oceans and old trees
Envelopes and allures
In this lonely place

We drink freely in the summer sun

Tawny, the leaves now
But they still hold

I know you
You are light in dreams
Precious as gold
Corn and oak

With fall of the first leaf
That winds rend,
In the woods alone
One must have the mind of winter
And I have been cold a long time

From Where Does It Come?

from where does it come
this thing that has moved with a fist of unreason
around my heart

with a touch of a hand
sounds turn on and off   and the room dark
in my storm of thuds and clacking in the night

past love to mania
the sole way to exist

hold   hard   then   hold hard

In My Garden

i have tried to grow violets and creeping
green vines on windowsills
and have a green thumb, when i remember
to water
strange, considering i'm a biologist first
then a biochemist and love to study
the intricacies of living things
trying to approximate truth
and have a laboratory filled with machines
and instruments to measure growth
i tend to a garden of cells in incubators
sometimes i daydream of the day
when i can tend a garden
envision swirling Impressionist colors
of purples and blues and greens
to dream in the serenity of nature
as i recall the days of my frenzied chase

Narrowing

choices constrict
like
glistening pebbles deep within
pearls

truly lovelorn
wrapped by layers   layers
until   opaque

i open myself
        to you
opalescent
shelling thin layer, one by one
until sheer with time

Órga Leannán (Golden Lover)

you came this time
exclaiming
      "i'm no false lover "

and wanted to wrap me warm
in russet blankets
lull me to sleep

your voice haunts me
as i drive along the Hudson
covered   in burnt oranges   browns

even when the silver sharp crackle of rain
and lightening   breaks
i know we have worn each other
like clothes from another time

the blush of winter on my lips
and bare branches
now hint of your parting
once lover entwined

Porcelain

as i sleep   your eyes are deep in
color
one   that i do not know   but there you lie
whirlpools of despair pull me

night skin cracks
thin lines in porcelain

Snow Angels

i asked
        "have you ever made snow angels"

i remembered
while making lasagna
watching the swirls of sauce
curl about the spoon
like snow on arms

Sought Music *Ex Nihilo*

(On listening to Musica Ricercata- György Ligeti)

each movement sought to enclose a new note
i do not want to escape
the room unfolds into a fugue
as your fingers gently searched
chords   blending   repeating one note then two……..

the air has hushed

Spirit Line

The People searched for dragonflies
yet found
spirit lines
splendor of red rock vortexes

ancient woven stories cry
                "they will lead us to water"

i find myself   dizzy
in this Flagstaff inn built with red brick

was it the altitude   or   was it my claiming
a break in the design

Wandering Men

summer
brings flies
above wandering men
who live their seconds
on concrete benches
watching

endless child's play
and grass stained Madonna
carrying their dead hopes
in her womb

Winter is the Reason

In the Village Bistro, only a few hours before midnight, pink and blue balloons hang down from the ceiling on silvery threads. Jazz goes on and on, three saxophones, drums, bass, piano and one lone singer softly out of tune but lovely to look at while the approaching new year comes in with a haze. It is so cold. I wear rabbit muffs, warm on my ears while I walk. It is so cold, like the cold cold winters of Chicago. My brain hurts, cannot remember things. Memories are lost before I reach out to grab them, slip between my cold fingers like tiny snowflakes on a night like this. I avoid looking in mirrors.

§§

> he did not write but meant
> one who is plagued with
> the syntax of things
> can never wholly kiss,
> desire

§§

> i try to remember
> gold snow angels
> photographed
> in Rockefeller Center

§§

> in bed, we tenderly
> hold our kiss
> through the night

§§

my brain hurts,   a
son, 28yrs and 130lbs
and 5' 10" died in his sleep

the autopsy will read:
cause of death induced
at birth by maternal neglect

my brain hurts

§§

All things are possible, like a full moon calling a doe to ponder her breath. Yet my belly aches.

New York Postcards

1
it is   11am as i walk
on the warm 34th St sidewalk
thinking   life always waits for me
at the edge of
rose petals

2
you once said
   "poetry saved my life"

in my impatience
barely audible, i asked
a woman in Barnes & Noble
   "where is the poetry section"

3
i once heard
that a complete life
was written on the back
of a postcard
only 600 words

quickly i walked
into a souvenir shop
darkly quiet on 42nd

then

selected a card

Holding a Pear

1
my love
is like holding a pear
as the stilled aroma
frames your lips
there is always
uncertainty
in ripeness
i offer this wholeness
for your awakening
so that you
may hold me
and taste
sweetness

2
i wait
an eternity
on the shelf or
from a bowl on the table
to be favored
they pass me by
i am too hard
or not hip enough for the season
i do not care
if it is a careless caressing

3
there is something pleasing
when a pear is eaten
the taste is delicate
not belonging to this world
it is not the stinging tartness of an orange
or bland sweetness of a red apple
it can be exotic in its display
but to most
an ordinary object
for view, placed just so in fruit bowls
maybe to be painted
maybe to be touched

Parties

tonight, i went to one of those parties
that is mixed with so much irony
it hurts.
i was telling a woman
(who is going to write for the New York Times)
that my daughter is beautiful
and she says, "i can tell, so are you." and i thought,
how much i would rather be at home reading.
so, i hung out in the kitchen
eating strawberries and whipped cream
with the hired help, listening to the Beatles,
waiting for a quick exit.

but i also thought,
how acutely aware
i have become
more entrenched in poetry.

so, how fucking
great is that?

About the Author

Karen Hubbard lived her early years in the Chicago area and is currently a Professor of Biology at The City College of New York and has published extensively in research areas of cancer and aging. She lives in West Orange, New Jersey. Since coming to New Jersey, she has given readings in several venues such as the Poet's Forum, the West Orange Arts Council Art Expo and Watchung Booksellers. She has published poetry in *Amelia, A Stone Unturned (Anthology), Austin Downtown Arts Magazine, Maultrommel, Open Doors (Anthology), Promethean, and Shot Glass Journal.* Her first book of poetry, *Rain,* was published in 2006.

www.ingramcontent.com/pod-product-compliance
Lightning Source LLC
Chambersburg PA
CBHW031635160426
43196CB00006B/430